AIR
POLLUTION

Heather C. Hudak

www.av2books.com

AV² provides enriched content that supplements and complements this book. Weigl's AV² books strive to create inspired learning and engage young minds in a total learning experience.

Your AV² Media Enhanced books come alive with...

Audio
Listen to sections of the book read aloud.

Key Words
Study vocabulary, and complete a matching word activity.

Video
Watch informative video clips.

Quizzes
Test your knowledge.

Go to **www.av2books.com**, and enter this book's unique code.

Embedded Weblinks
Gain additional information for research.

Slide Show
View images and captions, and prepare a presentation.

BOOK CODE

Z482594

AV² by Weigl brings you media enhanced books that support active learning.

Try This!
Complete activities and hands-on experiments.

... and much, much more!

Published by AV² by Weigl
350 5th Avenue, 59th Floor
New York, NY 10118
Website: www.av2books.com   www.weigl.com

Copyright ©2013 AV² by Weigl
All rights reserved. No part of this publication may be reproduced, stored in a retrieval system, or transmitted in any form or by any means, electronic, mechanical, photocopying, recording, or otherwise, without the prior written permission of the publisher.

Library of Congress Control Number: 2012941650
ISBN 978-1-61913-096-8 (hard cover)
ISBN 978-1-61913-543-7 (soft cover)

Printed in the United States of America in North Mankato, Minnesota
1 2 3 4 5 6 7 8 9 16 15 14 13 12

062012
WEP170512

Editor Aaron Carr
Design Ken Clarke

Every reasonable effort has been made to trace ownership and to obtain permission to reprint copyright material. The publishers would be pleased to have any errors or omissions brought to their attention so that they may be corrected in subsequent printings.

Weigl acknowledges Getty Images as its primary image supplier for this title.

CONTENTS

Eco Notes

One major form of air pollution is soot. Soot is made up of tiny pieces of dirt and grime that enter the air as smoke from burning fuel. Some common sources of soot are burning coal and diesel fuel. While it is in the air, soot absorbs heat from the Sun and increases the temperature of the **atmosphere**. Fortunately, soot is heavier than air, so it eventually falls back to the ground. Soot pollution can be reduced by using cleaner-burning fuels or filtering the smoke from existing fuels.

Studying Air Pollution

Clean air is important for life on Earth. In the past few hundred years, the quality of Earth's air has become a problem. **Toxic chemicals**, gases, and smoke particles from factories and cars pollute the air. This is called air pollution. Some air pollution comes from nature. The wind blows dust and dirt. Plants scatter pollen, and ocean waves spray salt. However, people cause more air pollution than nature. Polluted air can make people, plants, and animals ill.

Some air pollution is invisible. Smog is air pollution that can be seen. It is a yellowish-brown haze that hangs over some cities. Air pollution occurs all around the world. It can be found at home or in offices. It can be found in busy cities or in remote areas, such as the Arctic.

■ Factories, mills, and power plants spew billions of tons (tonnes) of pollution into the air each year.

What Causes Air Pollution?

Air pollution is everywhere. People burn fossil fuels to run vehicles, factories, and power plants. Fossil fuels include coal, gas, and oil. When fossil fuels are burned, smoke and chemicals are added to the air. **Greenhouse gases**, such as carbon dioxide, carbon monoxide, and sulfur dioxide, are produced when fossil fuels are burned. These gases are called air pollutants.

■ About 35 percent of all electric power around the world is made by burning coal. However, burning coal to make electricity releases carbon dioxide and other greenhouse gases into the air.

Effects of Air Pollution

Air pollution has many different effects. Some of the most common effects are smog, acid rain, and ocean acidification.

ACID RAIN

When sulfur dioxide from power plants mixes with water droplets in the air, the rain that falls is acid rain. Acid rain can harm the **environment**. It makes water unsafe for fish. Soil becomes poisoned. Buildings **corrode**. Acid rain can be carried by the wind for hundreds of miles (kilometers).

SMOG

Smog is fog mixed with chemicals and fumes that people who live in cities with a great deal of smog may have trouble breathing.

OCEAN ACIDIFICATION

Some gases that pollute the atmosphere dissolve in the ocean. This gradually increases the acidity of ocean waters. Over time, this acidic water dissolves the shells of animals such as corals and shellfish. This can destroy fragile coral reefs, and shut down fisheries.

Air Quality

People can find out how dirty or clean the air is where they live by checking the Air Quality Index (AQI). Each day, five major air pollutants are measured. Then, the local air quality is reported in the newspaper and on radio and television weather reports. It is even posted on the internet. The AQI also describes health problems that result from pollution. AQI is measured on a scale of 0 to 500. Three hundred is a high AQI. A high AQI means there is a large amount of air pollution. A low AQI means air pollution is not harmful to health. An AQI of 50 or below is thought to be low.

■ The average vehicle releases 5.6 tons (5.1 tonnes) of carbon dioxide into the air each year.

Air Quality Index

The AQI is divided into six categories. Each category is a different color. These colors are symbols for the level of health concern on a given day.

Green means the air is good. There are few, if any, health problems.

Yellow means the air quality is satisfactory. Still, some people may have problems breathing.

Orange means that people with certain health problems, such as heart or lung disease, are at risk. Most people will not be harmed by this air.

Red is the symbol for unhealthy air. Many people may be harmed by the air. Some people may have major problems.

Purple indicates that the air is very unhealthy. Many people may have major problems when air pollution levels are this high.

Maroon means the air is very harmful to all people. It may cause emergencies in some places.

The Ozone Layer

The ozone layer is part of Earth's atmosphere. It floats 10 to 30 miles (16 to 48 km) above the ground. The ozone layer protects people, plants, and animals from the Sun's harmful rays. It covers the entire Earth. Air pollution has caused the ozone layer to become thinner. As the ozone is destroyed, more of the Sun's rays reach Earth.

Chlorofluorocarbons (CFCs) are harmful chemicals that leak into the air and damage the ozone layer. CFCs are found in some cleaners, foam packing, and cooling liquids used in air conditioners and refrigerators. Many countries have stopped using CFCs, but damage has already been done to the ozone layer. In order for the ozone layer to be fully restored, humans will have to avoid causing any more damage for many years.

■ Chlorofluorocarbons (CFCs) are found in many everyday products, such as styrofoam packaging.

Earth's Shield

The ozone layer is thinnest above the South Pole in Antarctica. Here, the nights are very long and cold. At night, CFCs become trapped in ice crystals.

Cold causes CFCs to break down into smaller parts. One part is chlorine. Chlorine is especially damaging to the ozone layer. When the Sun rises, it thaws the ice crystals. Chlorine is released into the air, where it weakens Earth's shield against the Sun's **ultraviolet (UV) rays**.

Some plants and animals are harmed by too many UV rays. In oceans, big fish eat shrimp and krill. These tiny creatures shrivel up if exposed to too much UV light. This will leave no food for the big fish to eat. On land, plants are food for animals to eat. Too much UV light makes plants grow more slowly, so animals will have less food to eat.

Air Pollution Around the World

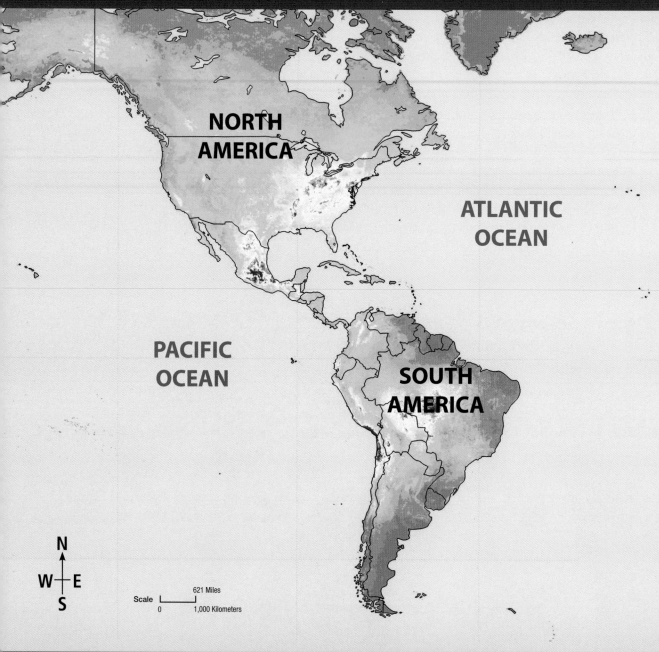

NORTH
AMERICA

ATLANTIC
OCEAN

PACIFIC
OCEAN

SOUTH
AMERICA

N
W—E
S

Scale

621 Miles

0   1,000 Kilometers

0   5   10   15   20   50   80   110

Fine **Aerosol** Pollution [micrograms/meter³]

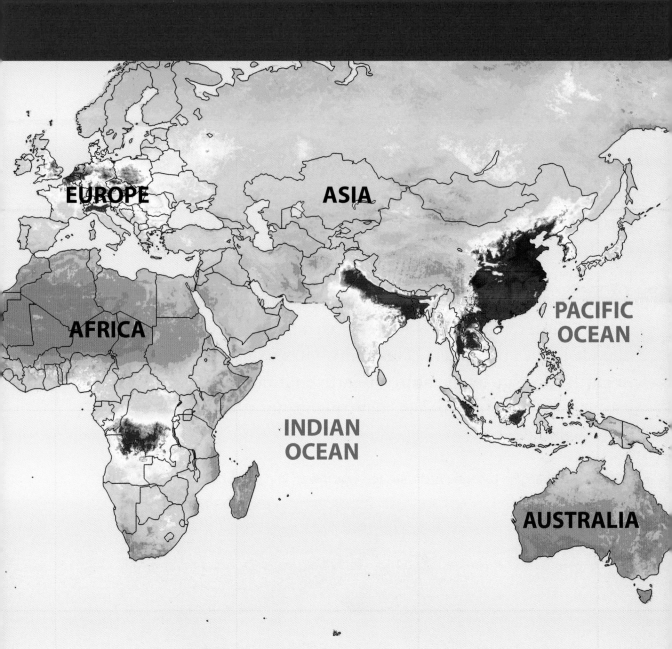

EUROPE

ASIA

AFRICA

PACIFIC
OCEAN

INDIAN
OCEAN

AUSTRALIA

SOUTHERN OCEAN

WHAT HAVE YOU LEARNED ABOUT AIR POLLUTION?

This map shows the areas most affected by air pollution. Use this map, and research in the library and online, to answer these questions.

1. Which continents are the largest polluters? Do these match up with the red areas of the map?

2. What forces move air pollution around the world?

Climate Change

Earth is gradually becoming warmer. This change in Earth's temperature is called climate change. Human activity is a major cause of climate change.

The major causes of climate change are greenhouse gases in Earth's atmosphere. Carbon dioxide is one of these gases. The gases in Earth's atmosphere trap the Sun's energy. They stop heat from releasing into space. Without this, Earth would be too cold to support many forms of life. However, over the last two centuries, humans have used more fossil fuels, such as coal and oil. Burning these fuels has increased the levels of carbon dioxide in the atmosphere. This contributes to an increase in Earth's average temperature. If Earth continues to become warmer, it will harm humans, many plants, most animals, and many **habitats**.

■ Climate change is reducing Arctic sea ice, which is an important habitat for polar bears.

Effects of Climate Change

Climate change may alter the way Earth looks. It can also cause health problems. Some changes in weather patterns can be traced to climate change. It can even change the food people eat.

 **HURRICANES** Climate change is causing tropical seas to warm. The heat creates more energy. This increased energy means hurricanes may become stronger.

 **HEALTH** Hot weather causes health problems. Some people become sick from heat stress. Young children and seniors are most at risk.

 **HABITATS** Sudden changes in temperature may harm habitats. In the past, temperature changes were usually slow. Plants and animals had time to become used to the change. This may not be true in the future.

 **FLOODING** Climate change is causing **glaciers** to melt. Water is rising all over the world. Coastlines may flood.

 **FOOD SUPPLY** Climate change may cause **droughts**. Too much heat could cause plants to die. It may also dry up ponds and other sources of water used for crops. Areas that are already dry may become deserts.

The Environment

Today, many people are trying to save the environment. They know that it is important to have clean air. Some governments have made laws that limit how much pollution companies can produce.

Scientists have made cleaner fuels. Natural gas, alcohol, and batteries are just a few examples of cleaner energy sources. Most car builders put catalytic converters in cars. Catalytic converters attach to the **exhaust** pipe. They reduce the amount of pollutants that are released into the air.

■ Electric cars have rechargeable batteries that can power the car up to 120 miles (190 km).

Fossil fuels are made from the remains of plants and animals that lived long ago in Earth's history. Over millions of years, plants pulled carbon dioxide from the atmosphere, and stored it in their bodies. When these plants died, they were buried under ground. Over time, heat and pressure changed them into fossil fuels. Fossil fuels are being created very slowly. It takes 50 to 250 million years for fossil fuels to form. Some scientists think that humans have consumed as much as half of all the fossil fuels that currently exist on Earth.

Preventing Air Pollution

There are many ways to help prevent air pollution. Planting trees, using less energy for daily activities, and reducing waste are all ways people can help reduce air pollution.

PLANTING TREES

Trees draw carbon dioxide from the atmosphere in order to grow. They also absorb sunlight and store it as chemical energy instead of heat.

RIDING BIKES

Bicycles are one of the most energy-efficient machines invented by humans. Riding a bike or walking to school does not burn fossil fuels. It also helps people stay healthy.

FIND WAYS TO USE LESS ENERGY

One of the best things you can do for the environment is reducing waste. This not only means throwing fewer things away, but not using what you do not need. Turning down the thermostat in your home and using energy-efficient light bulbs are just a few ways to do this. Energy-efficient light bulbs need to be properly recycled, and should not be thrown out with the garbage.

Air Pollution Indoors

Air pollution is not just outdoors. It can be inside, too. Hairspray and cleaners are some of the pollutants people use indoors. Dust, pet fur, and **dander** also cause air pollution.

People can become ill from breathing air pollutants. Lungs clean the air we breathe, but over time, pollutants can damage lungs. Breathing then becomes difficult or painful.

■ Studies have shown that people spend up to 90 percent of their time indoors. Other studies indicate that indoor air is often more polluted than outdoor air in large cities. This means that, for many people, indoor air pollution causes greater health risks than outdoor air pollution.

What is a Climatologist?

Climatologists are scientists who study long-term trends in Earth's climate, such as global warming. They are like detectives who try to find answers and solve problems.

Climatologists look at how climate is affected by many factors. It could be affected by plants and animals, by how people use the land, or by pollution. Climatologists take measurements on the ground, in oceans, and in the air. They even study **ice cores** taken from glaciers to learn how Earth's climate may have changed in the past. Climatologists put all of these measurements into computers to predict how Earth's climate might change in the future.

Michael E. Mann

Michael E. Mann specializes in the study of Earth's climate in the past. After earning his PhD from Yale University, he joined a group of elite scientists studying climate change for the International Panel on Climate Change. In 2007, he was one of many scientists presented with the Nobel Peace Prize for this work. Today, he is the director of the Earth System Science Center at Pennsylvania State University.

ICE CORES

Every year, a new layer of ice and snow builds up on the world's glaciers. An ice core is a long stack of all these layers. By counting the layers, scientists can find the age of the glacier. These layers of ice also trap gases from the atmosphere. By studying these gases, climatologists can tell what Earth's atmosphere was like long ago.

Six Facts About Air Pollution

A major study found that air pollution was worse in Sequoia National Park than in cities such as Atlanta, New York, and Houston.

Recent cars create less air pollution than those built 40 years ago. One car made in the 1960s produced as much pollution as 20 new cars today.

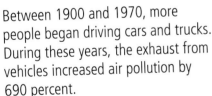

Between 1900 and 1970, more people began driving cars and trucks. During these years, the exhaust from vehicles increased air pollution by 690 percent.

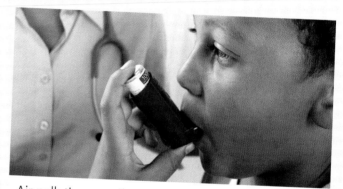

Air pollution contributes to **asthma**. Between 1980 and 1996, the number of asthmatic Americans rose by 74 percent.

A killer smog hit London, England, in 1952. After four days of smog, 12,000 people died. As a result, laws were made to restrict the kinds and amounts of pollution allowed into the air.

Not all electric cars are better for the environment. If the electricity comes from a coal-burning power plant, a gasoline-powered car may be cleaner.

Air Pollution Brain Teasers

1 What is air pollution?

2 How many new cars would it take to make as much air pollution as one 1960s car?

3 Where does most air pollution come from?

4 Name two fossil fuels.

5 What is smog?

6 What does the Air Quality Index measure?

7 What is the thin layer of atmosphere that protects people, plants, and animals from the Sun's harmful rays?

8 What is causing the ozone layer to become thinner?

9 Where do chlorofluorocarbons (CFCs) come from?

10 Which type of scientist studies climate change?

ANSWERS: 1. Toxic chemicals, gases, and smoke particles that pollute the air 2. 20 new cars 3. From human activity 4. Coal, gas, or oil 5. Chemicals and fumes that gather in the air and mix with fog 6. The amount of pollution in the air where people live 7. The ozone layer 8. Greenhouse gases 9. CFCs are used in some cleaners, foam packing, and cooling liquids used in refrigerators and air conditioners. They leak into the air. 10. A climatologist

Science in Action

Test for Air Pollutants

This activity should be done with an adult.

Tools Needed

penny

4 petri dishes

microscope

4 microscope slides

wax pencil

petroleum jelly

masking tape

Directions

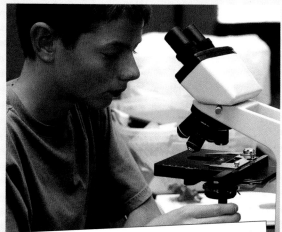

1 Place the penny on a slide. Trace around the penny with the wax pencil. Rub petroleum jelly inside the circle. Repeat for all slides.

2 Put one slide in each petri dish. Place the four dishes around the classroom. Stick a piece of tape to the side of each petri dish. Write the name of each location on the tape.

3 Collect the dishes after two days. Look through the microscope at the particles stuck to the petroleum jelly on each slide.

4 Count the number of particles on each dish. Did one area of your classroom have more pollution than the others? Why do you think this might be?

Key Words

aerosol: the fine particles of liquid or solid dispensed from a spray can

asthma: a lung disease that makes breathing difficult

atmosphere: the layer of gases around Earth

corrode: to wear away slowly

dander: flaky scales of skin, feathers, or fur

droughts: long periods of time without rain

environment: the objects and conditions that make a place what it is

exhaust: smoke or gas from an engine

glaciers: large masses of ice

greenhouse gases: gases that reflect heat back to Earth

habitats: places where a plant or animal lives in nature

ice cores: samples of glacier ice

toxic chemicals: poisons

ultraviolet (UV) rays: rays from the Sun

Index

Log on to www.av2books.com

AV[2] by Weigl brings you media enhanced books that support active learning. Go to www.av2books.com, and enter the special code found on page 2 of this book. You will gain access to enriched and enhanced content that supplements and complements this book. Content includes video, audio, weblinks, quizzes, a slide show, and activities.

Audio
Listen to sections of the book read aloud.

Video
Watch informative video clips.

Embedded Weblinks
Gain additional information for research.

Try This!
Complete activities and hands-on experiments.

WHAT'S ONLINE?

Try This!	Embedded Weblinks	Video	EXTRA FEATURES
Complete a waste reduction activity. Identify the types of air pollution. Try an air pollution mapping activity. Test your knowledge of air pollution.	Learn more about air pollution. Find Air Quality Index ratings for your area. Read more about climate change. Learn more about how reducing waste and energy use can help the environment.	Watch a video about air pollution. Watch a video about climate change.	**Audio** Listen to sections of the book read aloud. **Key Words** Study vocabulary, and complete a matching word activity. **Slide Show** View images and captions, and prepare a presentation. **Quizzes** Test your knowledge.

AV[2] was built to bridge the gap between print and digital. We encourage you to tell us what you like and what you want to see in the future.

Sign up to be an AV[2] Ambassador at www.av2books.com/ambassador.